RADIANT
JUKEBOX

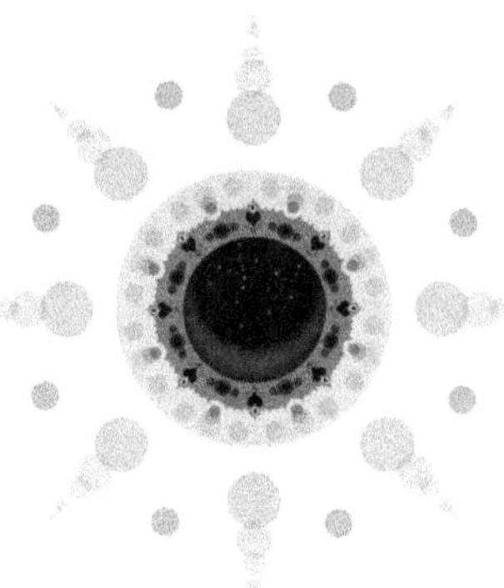

RADIANT JUKEBOX

POEMS

BECKY VENTURA

Cover Art: John Regier Claassen
Section Openers: *Winter Aspect/Moondala*: Jillian Marie Ventura
Promenade: Art Work *Water Plains:* Patricia Ritchie
Author Photo: Lifetouch National Photography Studios

Editor: Judyth Hill
Proofreader: Barbara Erdody
Book Design: Mary M. Meade

ISBN 979 8718971811

Raise your words, not your voice.

It is rain that grows flowers, not thunder.

—Mevlânâ Jalāl ad-Dīn Muhammad Rūmī
translated by
Reza Rostamzadeh Khosroshahi

CONTENTS

PART 1

IMPROVISATIONS

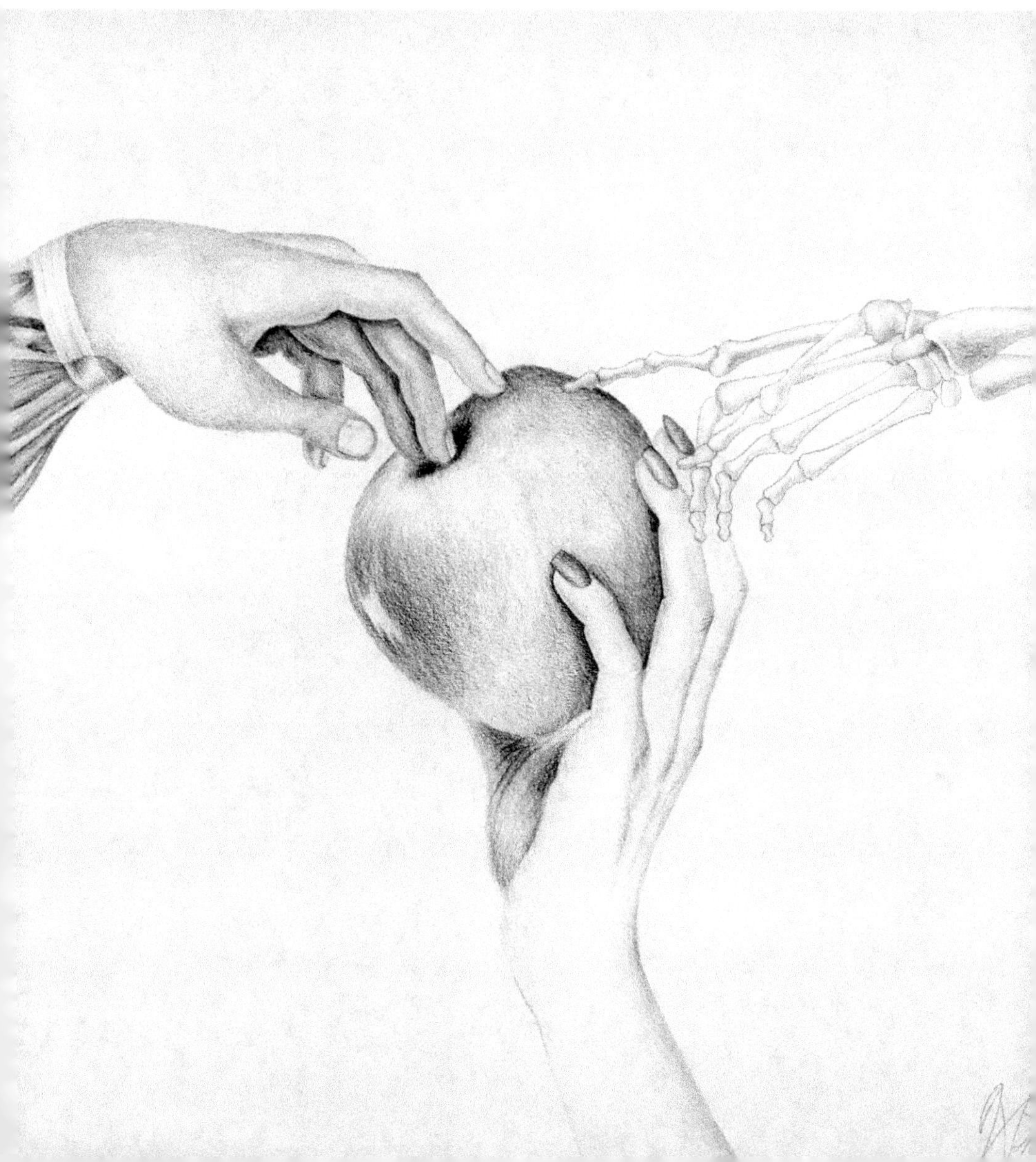

Der Tee Meiner Grossmutter

Cool and smooth in my hands
Small stain on the spout
   where tea has dripped
   rubs off with a finger.

Small flecks and cracks
   gone unnoticed
Gold etching, slightly worn
Royal Albert China, England.

I spent the night at Grandma's
   stayed up late reading
   Rosechen and the Wicked Magpie
Grandma came in.

"Oh, I shouldn't have
   given you that tea," she said.
The next morning
I learned to like scrambled eggs.

Burgundy background

    bone white flowers, blue in the center,

This teapot holds memories,

and yes, tea.

Mary Catherine

I carried you down the beach

    on a brilliant mid-summer day.

    You fastened yourself to me like a brooch.

I listen to you talk,

    my attention undivided,

    laughing, crying sometimes.

You told me how you left school

    when you were in first grade,

    the teacher sent you to the principal's office.

Instead, you skipped home,

    told your grandmother they let you go home early,

    because you were a good little girl.

You were not only

    a naughty little girl,

    but a liar to boot.

No, you're a clown, a merrymaker,

    belting out "I've Got a Gal in Kalamazoo,"

    a streetwalker in the *Madwoman of Chaillot*.

You made carmen-skirted dolls from hollyhocks,

daydreamed about fancy formal dances,

changed your little brother's diaper.

Non-competitive gamer, Earth Shoe wearer, recycler,

"I-message" spouting, macgyveresque non-conformist.

That's you.

You became a butterfly I carried down the beach,

and placed tenderly

on a bed of wildflowers.

Down the Rabbit Hole

She wanted to write, but didn't know how.

She followed her mind to a dark alley
    but ran out quickly.

Mourning dove chose a sunny branch,
    her mate, nearby, holding space.

Tremulous leaves, autumn bliss embodied,
    lose their grip one by one.

She munches her biscuit.

Cardinal nibbles seed,
    Chickadee stops by to console.

Everybody leaves,
    yet they are still there.

Fugitive Visions

Don't put this on like an old shoe.

It is not meant to be comfortable.

It is not meant to be predictable.

Maybe you will feel different…

instead of falling into

Expectation's arms.

There was a love in your dream who was

someone you detested.

There was a love in your dream who was

not available.

There are questions, mysteries, untapped strengths,

brilliant gemstones, or diamonds in the rough,

Cyrano's prose, or Cyrano's nose?

She Pontificates at the Podium

"All will be well, this blip of time will pass.

Do your dharma, my loves.

Touching your toes may not help you, but certainly

breathing deeply and slowly will, my dears."

"And at night when you cannot sleep

(perhaps a centipede fell from the air vent onto your sheets!)

laugh and remember those you love

and pray for those who are difficult to love."

"All will be well. I feel it in my bones.

Do your dharma, my loves.

Fill out postcards, send texts, put one foot in front of the other.

Go to your street corner with your sign;
    take a knee for nine minutes."

"All will be well. Evil is exposed.

You are learning much about the company you keep.

We clean house and move on.

This is how we stretch and grow."

"Remember, this is but a blip of time that seems never-ending.

Do your dharma, my loves.

Write your poems. Play your music.

Allow your wild heart to guide you on this journey."

Winter Aspect

Snow falling

manna from heaven

hope's gift,

    heart-healing balm.

Gray sky

warm comfort

chorus of frozen flakes

    quietly sounding within.

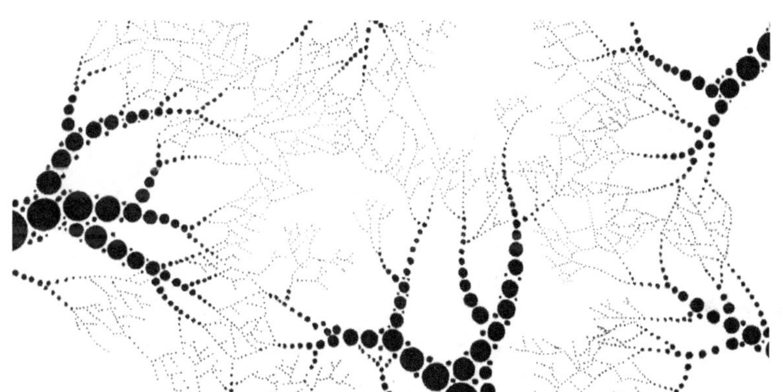

A Musing

Muse, come sit on my shoulder.

No, that's not how it works.
I come as I please,
I go as I please.
Maybe it will be today,
    perhaps in the future....
Don't consider me too deeply!
I have my ways.....

Muse, I love you....
I love how you visit me when I'm at the piano
    playing Schumann or Bach....
Especially Bach.

I know, I am there.
More than you know.
Just let me in,
    try not to think too hard
    and I'll be there.

I think you were there the other night,

   but then I lost you

   before I picked up my pen....

I suppose that brilliant thing is still within....

Oh, indeed, it is.

First Arabesque

Adorable Arabesque, *très expressif*

melodies intertwine

    like two lovers in rapture.

Unpretentious, lovely lines of expression

    vite.......sans retinir,

watery, ivory ebb and flow.

Delicate arpeggios,

authoritative chords

    sing heart prayers, cavernous, internal.

Graceful passages drift upward,

pause for what seems eternity....

Repose for a travel-worn soul.

*Un peu moins vite....*which path to take?

Off we go again...charmingly, simply, easily,

navigating, pausing, considering.

Now! With resolution!

Return, in a lacey spiral to the familiar,

to meet our beloved once more.

Freely dive

soar, high

climb to unknown peaks, higher…

and……

shhhhhhhh!

Doux Repos

Kensington

A MetroPark in Milford, Michigan

Majestically strutting on spindly legs,

    scarlet-headed beauty with warning hiss.

Shadowy stumps that move

    block the roadway; let them pass.

Human bird feeder, hand outstretched,

    St. Francis of Assisi smiles.

Downy One gently picks up seed;

    he leaves no hole behind.

He lost his eye, still he could see,

    he lost his eye, and could not trust.

Dappled sunlight, cool green scent.

Chirring chipmunks chase each other.

Mother Nature reveals her palette.

Mother Nature performs her composition.

In attendance: wild turkey, tufted tit,

    bold little woodpecker, sandhill crane.

INSPIRATIONS

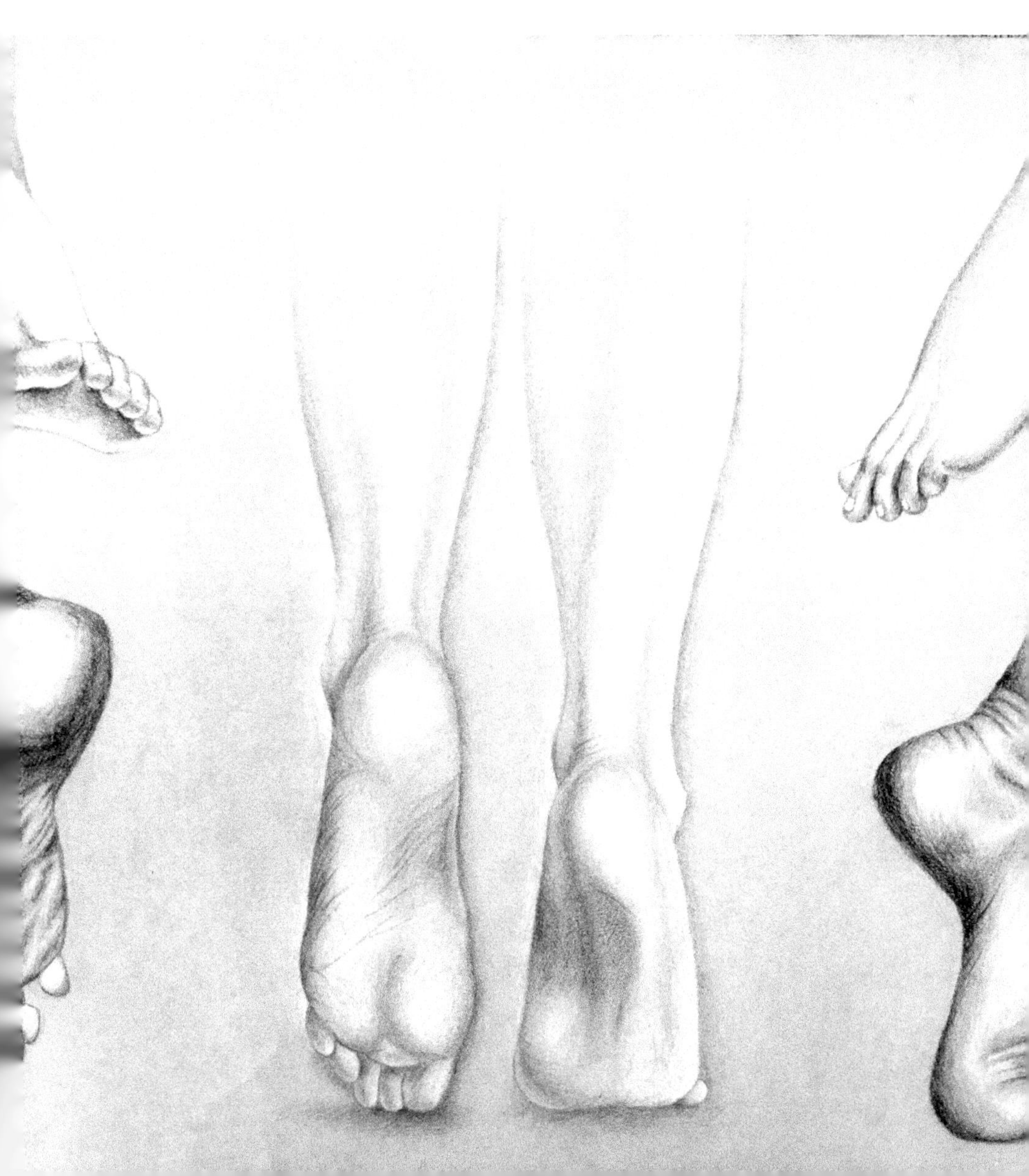

Nature

Inspired by André Breton: "Free Union"

Nature with cumulus cirrus hair

Nature with blue spacious hair

Nature's neck of pearls, neck of jet streams' lazy paths

Nature with teeth of a bear and tiger skin cushion.

Nature with teeth that bite, jaws that snap and snarl.

Nature with eyes that look

Nature with eyes that burn

Hot fury, stinging, piercing wild-blue flame.

Nature with a scarf on her shoulder,
scarf of white on her shoulder.

Cotton-white on her shoulder, soft, flowing fringe.

Nature with her arms,

Nature with embracing arms, arms with bangles,
arms that bind.

Arms that break free; Nature's arms.

Nature with her mind, kind mind, free mind,
mind of her own.

Nature with hips. Nature with earthquake hips.

Nature with rolling thunder hips, volcano hips.

Nature with legs of bark and tree stumps, apple groves,

Nature with wine vineyards.

Nature with songs, birdsongs, radio blasts with laughter.

Nature with music.

Nature sighing,

Nature with wind gently blowing, zephyr sweeping,

quaking aspens and mighty oaks, whispering sweet nothings.

Nature rests, in quietude, in solitude; spins out comfort.

Nature with cumulus cirrus hair.

Nature with blue cyan spacious hair, scarf on her neck.

Nature with a cool, cotton-white scarf on her neck.

She

Inspired by John Ashbery: "He"

She is the gold dust on a field of marigolds.

She is the pyramid's pinnacle.

She is the boulder that ran downhill laughing

She is the fire and flame that burn inside.

She gives freely until there is no more

She does as she wishes with abandon

She needs no one and lives in a cave. Sometimes

She loves, she hates; she cries, she laughs.

She goes in, within

She goes out, finding you

She celebrates

She is all-knowing, not understanding anything.

She is old and wise, young and foolish

She hides her pain; she shares her feelings

She lives for nature

She throws away garbage.

She has anxiety

She runs around like a chicken, head off

She has it together, but not

She is strong, she cries at night wondering

She runs away then runs back

She buys useless items she likes

She makes a clay pot, fills it with nothing

She shakes out her hands and legs. Nothing falls

She is loved by everyone – she thinks so

She has sinned

She can't bear it

She finds joy in contentment.

She is hovering near for so long now

She has butterfly's wings, flying

She writes her stories. They are here still

She clowns with a bright suit and face paint, then left the
    building.

She didn't lose well, so cheated

She smiled and forgot

She set a fabulous table

She made him dinner, but he died. Watching "Lassie."

She comes, and she goes.

She is me, but she is not me.

She knows things

She never shared.

She is a hero; she has flaws

She is part of humanity

She cries, screams, laughs, giggles, jumps, reclines, cajoles

She has fear and courage, she is finite and infinite.

I'mpressions

Inspired by N. Scott Momaday: "The Delight Song of Tsoai-talee"

I am fishing for lightning trumpets,

thunder flashes, then sleeps.

I am chanting, glittering, rocket-like

exploding, snapping, wide open!

I am green with peace,

emerald leaves make my sweater.

I am exhaling a string of thoughts

tatted in Victorian lace.

I am as a spider, waiting,

at midnight, legs curled in my sycamore web.

I am a puddle of yellow,

butter melts, oozing with golden delight.

I am spinning out poetry of another kind

poems with no words flow out.

I am afloat on lilac fragrance,

inner wisdom's bubbles surface.

I am a thousand faces peering from windows
I am the whole dream of these things.

Recitativ

Inspired by Billy Collins: "Litany"

I am a circle of stones

strong and clever

hugging the ground.

You are scarlet, emerald,

wild twisted colors

from your dreams.

I am not the blind woman's teacup,

feral cat under the porch,

or toothpaste speck on the mirror.

You are not

a slow dance in the evening,

or fresh-baked cinnamon rolls.

I am free to be thunder,

mad and loud,

or quiet rainwater.

Take a *quick look in the mirror.*
You burn like a tiger
inside a hurricane.

I am not narrow in my thoughts

but listen, on occasion,

to the drummer within.

You are not narrow in your thoughts

you are candles in the window

and a roaring fireplace.

It might interest you to know…
Lilac-sweet fragrances gust through the door,

and pale spider's webs glisten in moonlight.

It also might interest you to know
that anyone can dance

alone in darkness.

Promenade

Curiosity went for a stroll in corners of dreams and images.

A tsunami of fire, born of rain, crashed down.

It was this day she was told she was a strong woman.

In her basket, a book that belongs to Abdullah, unwanted or forgotten.

Elephant-skin waters laugh at sand dunes, forms ever-changing.

Pull up a tree stump, take a load off your feet. Let's talk.

   A pencil left here, notes hastily scribbled stashed there…

   like finding a twenty in an old coat pocket.

Chase the ambulance, through red lights, heart tempo accelerates.

Scared of what's in there? Go back in. Abide within awhile.

> *Allow what's inside to be*
>
> *without question, poof!*
>
> *It blows away like ashes.*

Patricia Ritchie: *Water Plains*

Endearments

Inspired by Pablo Neruda: Love Sonnet XV

The earth has known you for a long time now

you are velvet moss that grows in shady darkness

   evergreen and ever soft

you are calmness in the face of despair.

This earth has known you, needs you

you are the music Saraswati plays

on the strings of her *veena,*

exotic, wild, unbound.

The earth has known you for a long time…yes….

Sierras, Rockies, Berkshires, Cascades

   wave and plead from afar: "Come back, come back to me….."

You are moon-glow and citrine-shine,

Van Gogh's night on canvas,

   brilliant, ebullient light-shimmer.

Celebration
Inspired by Walt Whitman: "Song of Myself"

Ride a bicycle, feel wind on skin, work the pedals.

Read a book; become deliciously, wondrously sleepy.

Savor sweet words from a friend after bringing a baked blueberry
handpie from the kitchen you dance in every day.

Stay inside, *homage au piano*, heart exposed.

Go outside, forest bathe, talk to deer.

Help Cass Corridor's downtrodden.

Send a postcard.

Write. Throw all caution to the wind.

Some things that ought to be expressed may be deeply buried.

Music, poetry and yoga sing the *Song of Myself,*

Over the tree-tops I float thee a song!

Teaching is a kindness, a calling, to help others help themselves.

Encourage. Acknowledge. Model. Wipe tears.

Playing Yahtzee with a 94-year-old is a time to cherish.

Any time with your 94-year-old father is time to cherish.

Again, and again, and again, follow the Goddess' Impulse.

Step joyously through the Thunderbolt Gate.

A Half-Baked Loafe

"I loafe and invite my soul" – Walt Whitman

Sitting with highballs in mid-day with neighbors

their old dog moans at midnight.

Wandering through shops, incense drifts,

saturating clothing.

Campfires blow smoke

crackling flames speak a language of their own.

Sitting still, sounds through the window caress

hum of machines, breeze through leaves, birds, cicadas, a dog's
    bark.

The phone rings, a grieving friend needs an ear

gratitude wells up for having time to give.

Groundhog made his appearance

lord of all he surveys, he waddles off.

They lined up….she let them…..

so they too could have bunnies on their papers.

Writing, once a duty, is now

a pleasure and an adventure.

A beautiful table laid, there were new potatoes,

butter, gravy, and always dessert.

"I think I have another turn," she said,

and they let her have it.

He took firewood to those raucous boys

she took cookies to new neighbors.

Pots of marigolds framed the porch

down these steps he fell in his wheelchair.

Tuesday, all the world's problems will be solved

well, at least Monday's.....

They ran, then he showed her how

to blow her nose without a handkerchief.

From rounder to tighter, smoother to rougher,

longer to shorter, oilier to drier…the toll of time…

Lingering by the lake, watching ducks' blue feathers shine

they come near, wanting to be fed.

Riding in a Tesla, music on or not

moonroof open, air, sounds, and scents envelop her.

Angel of Manifestation

her efforts, determination, and perseverance have paid off.

a) Shake it loose b) Let it go   c) Resist

d) Allow e) All of the Above

The Judges
Inspired by Kaylin Haught: "God Says Yes to Me"

Too short

they said.

Just right

I said.

Not enough detail

they said.

Too much

I said.

You don't know what you're doing

they said.

You got that right*

I said.

*Substitute your favorite retort here.

INVENTIONS

Trance Dance

Inspired by Hafez: "Ghazal 84"

Darkness surrounds us, dancing together.

Toss off our shackles, chancing together.

Hair tossing wildly, Nataraja aflame,

twist! Leap! Joyously prancing together.

Drums' carnal percussion, Spirit descends,

Shiva and Shakti romancing together.

Dervishes whirling, Goddesses swirling,

glittering visions we're glancing together.

Deep into Blackness, Mystery beckons,

sparkle, dance, flicker! Advancing, together.

Moondala Cento

Sat the lone singer wonderful causing tears.

When the moon comes up,

she sings as the moon sings.

I am also the moon in the trees,

a single moon drop in the grass,

and I still don't know if I am a falcon, or a storm, or a great song.

O moon do not keep her from me any longer

for beautiful you are, my world, my true…

I love you without knowing how, or when, or from where.

I never knew I liked the night pitch-black.

This way, and that, she peers, and sees,

the moon is her topaz eye.

The darkest evening of the year,

   all creation shivers,

and the heart feels like an island in infinity.

The soul, like the moon, is new, and always new again.

Marvel at the softness that still remains.

I rest in the grace of the world and am free.

Low-hanging moon! What is that dusky spot in your brown
   yellow?

Striped Gopher Looks Back Moon, the Assiniboine people say.

And they ought to know.

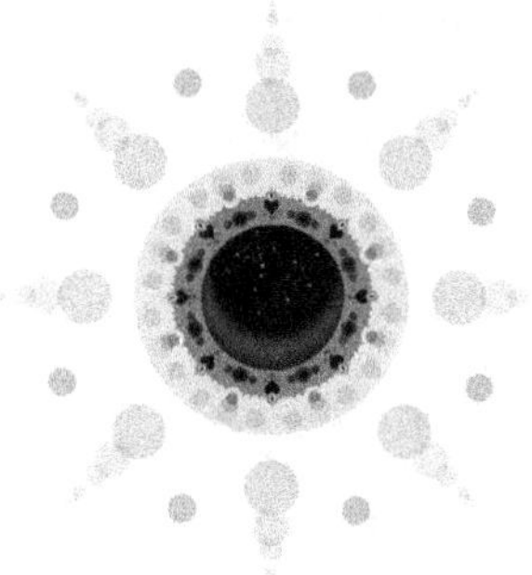

Ode to a Dutch Pump

A card with Dutch pump etched within
    meandered through the mail one day.
Not lost to some recycle bin
    lest sentiment slip away.

Rough-hewn wood-pump, cap atop,
fluid spout and handle-arm.
A trough for cows' and horses' slop,
sharp-needled conifers surround the farm.

Architect student, '48, to hear it,
a sketch saved from defection.
    "Little happenstances, profound presence of spirit,
    serve to keep our strong connection."

Water is life, oh blessed invention,
fitting model for our artist's pen.
Salutations, sincere, fulfill intention,
satisfied, till we thirst again.

DUTCH PUMP
CLAASSEN, J.R. ~ PLATE 16 ~ ARCH 202 (1)

A Respite from Their Usual Flight

Inspired by Dylan Thomas: "Do not go gentle into that good night"

A respite from their usual flight,

savoring seeds hid in the snow,

at blue jay's call, fly out of sight.

Cardinals amongst the sparrows light.

"We are one," they seem to know.

A respite from their usual flight.

Suet and nuts provide delight.

Silent alarm disrupts the flow,

at blue jay's call, fly out of sight.

Who dares to take that next bite?

Who dares stand against the foe?

A respite from their usual flight.

Brave ones peck with all their might.

Fear stirs on the ground below,

at blue jay's call, fly out of sight.

Others look from tree-limb height,

woodpeckers, tenacious, will not go.

A respite from their usual flight;

at blue jay's call, fly out of sight.

Visiting the Bird Feeder in Winter

Inspired by Robert Frost: "Stopping by Woods on a Snowy Evening"

Birds, in canon, land in snow.

Alarmed, they hasten now to go.

Blue jay cries: "It's all okay,"

    for he's on guard, and he should know.

The snow is white, the sky is gray,

much colder than the other day.

A pop of color, scarlet red,

cardinal takes one's breath away.

He quickly moves his little head,

the Downy One is being fed

suet is his great delight

as he pecks it to a shred.

Sparrows coming in, alight

when there's seed, there is a fight

fluttering wings, sharp beaks that bite

snatch some seed, and then take flight.

Sestina Siesta

Frenetically flying hummingbird
displaying throat of ruby.
What moves him? Perhaps chased
from allium, globe-thistle, geraniums,
by sounds of a bell;
tintinnabulations in a tantalizing tangle.

Driftwood, shipwreck, seaweed tangle.
Darting, quickly, like the hummingbird.
Walking, loving, laughing, hearing the bell
in the churchyard, she slips on her ruby
sweater and wanders past geraniums
smiling and content, blues chased.

Scents on the breeze, wind-chased.
Reminders activated by distant bell.
Vivid and glorious geraniums
with petals red as a ruby
or breast of a hummingbird
mingle in a fragrance-tangle.

In the pot of dirt, geraniums.

Lake-water shining like a ruby.

Freedom of flight: swift hummingbird,

now wings in a deadly tangle.

Into the fishline chased

then saved by the bell.

No alarms, no ringing bell.

In their prison pots, geraniums.

Freedom for sweet ruby-

throated bird, tiny hummingbird,

released from her line-tangle.

Heart still racing, as tho' chased.

Strands, strings, slimy tangle,

foamy waters waves have chased.

"Go to meeting," sounds the bell.

Trudging past geraniums,

in each ear, a ruby.

Rest peacefully, sweet hummingbird.

Hold the hummingbird as if a ruby.

Thoughts chased, now alive to geraniums.

Breezes and bell melt in a melodious tangle.

Molly's Pantoum

This is where you grow.

This is where you heal.

Dance life into each day.

Magic is the fuel for miracles.

This is where you heal,

nourish your wildest dreams.

Magic is the fuel for miracles,

you know the ones.

Nourish your wildest dreams,

keep looking up.

You know the ones,

laugh and play.

Keep looking up

to feel more alive.

Laugh and play!

Sit with the sunflowers.

To feel more alive,

dance life into each day.

Sit with the sunflowers,

this is where you grow.

Terza Rima

Terza Rima, a poetic form

has tercets with rhymes interlocking.

Most poets follow this norm.

Frost's poem, written while walking,

rhymes final stanza with first.

Dante, however, kept talking.

When WildWriting, immersed,

perhaps a slow write in a hiss,

or words jumping out in a burst.

Rhyme scheme for tercets is this:

aba, bcb, cdc, ded…..

Forever! It's poetic bliss.

So, poetry forms can be free,

or with boundaries for those who are yearning

the poem will decide how to be.

End it like Frost, if that's what you're
learning,

or maybe, like Dante, keep hellfire burning.

Aubade Triptych

No. 1

Mourning dove flew to the tree

Birdsong all around me

Cool dampish breeze

Hum of cicadas

Grass cool beneath my feet

Squirrel does a balancing act

He eyes me warily.

Perched cardinal turns his back on me,

Seed deposit!

No. 2

Birds in congress on the roof…

a launching pad of sorts as they decide:

feeder or lilac bush?

In sails woodpecker….

Yellow finch cocks his little head…

"Who are you?"

Kerfuffle above me, ah….

Squirrel again.

Jay interrupts, bossy fellow, head-tuft ruffled

screeches at the other birds.

Goldfinch ponders…

then flies off.

No. 3

Garden splendor!

Squash beginning to ripen

butterflies and bees, happy with their bounty

lovely hibiscus opening wide as an umbrella,

tongue sticking out, petals thin as paper.

Expansive field beyond the yard—

I am alone here

cocooned in sound.

Breeze-carried delights:

green scent, bee's perfume.

Two unmoving owl sentinels,

garden guards, usher me home.

Acknowledgments

I would like to thank Judyth Hill, my mentor and Poet Goddess, for her help in crafting *Radiant Jukebox.* Much gratitude goes to Mary Meade for her work designing and producing the final form of this book. My talented family and friends shared their artwork for this book: My father, John Claassen, created the book's cover and the sketch for "Ode to a Dutch Pump." My daughter, Jillian, created the artwork on the section pages, "Winter Aspect," and "Moondala." Patricia Ritchie, my dear friend, allowed me to use her artwork *Water Plains* for "Promenade." Her artwork is also in her children's book, *The Dunehaven Council.* I'm grateful for the support of my friends and family. I appreciate the Poetry Society of Michigan for providing an artistic forum. I'm also grateful for our Poetry Manuscript Clan: Judyth, Rosalynn, Lawton, Lorraine, Linda, Akira, Karen, Melinda, Kelly, Doris, and Lee, for sharing their experiences and insights and for keeping each other safely supported.

Poetry Quotes/Credits

"Nature" was inspired by André Breton's "Free Union," translated by Kenneth White.

"She" was inspired by John Ashbery's "He."

The line "I am the whole dream of these things" in "I'mpressions" is quoted from N. Scott Momaday's "The Delight Song of Tsoai-talee."

The lines "I am not the blind woman's teacup" and "It might (also) interest you to know" in "Recitativ" are quoted from Billy Collins' "Litany."

The line "The earth has known you for a long time now" in "Endearments" is quoted from Pablo Neruda's "Love Sonnet XV," translated by Stephen Tapscott.

The line "Over the tree-tops I float thee a song" in "Celebration" is quoted from Walt Whitman's "Song of Myself."

"A Half-Baked Loafe" was inspired by Walt Whitman's "Song of Myself."

"The Judges" was inspired by Kaylin Haught's "God Says Yes to Me."

"Moondala Cento" includes quotes, in the order they appear in the poem, from the following poets: Walt Whitman: "Out of the Cradle Endlessly Rocking," Federico Lorca: "La Luna Asoma" translated by William B. Logan, William Butler Yeats: "He and She," Billy Collins: "Litany," Pablo Neruda: "Love Sonnet XLVIII," translated by Stephen Tapscott, Rainer Maria Rilke: "Ich lebe mein Leben in wachsenden Ringen," translated by Robert Bly, Walt Whitman: "Out of the Cradle Endlessly Rocking," e.e. cummings: "i carry your heart with me (i carry it in)," Pablo Neruda: "Love Sonnet XVII," translated by Stephen Tapscott, Nazim Hikmet: "Things I Didn't Know I Loved," translated by Randy Blasing and Mutlu Konuk, Walter de la Mare: "Silver," G. Orr Clark: "The Night is a Big Black Cat," Robert Frost: "Stopping by Woods on a Snowy Evening," William Butler Yeats: "He and She," Federico Lorca: "La Luna Asoma," translated by William B. Logan, Lal Ded: "The Soul, Like the Moon," translated by Coleman Barks, Ellen Birkett Morris: "Abide," Wendell Berry: "The Peace of Wild Things," Walt Whitman: "Out of the Cradle Endlessly Rocking," Judyth Hill: "Moon in This Season."

"Trance Dance" was inspired by Hafez' "Ghazal 84," translated by Roger Sedarat.

"A Respite from Their Usual Flight" was inspired by Dylan Thomas' villanelle, "Do not go gentle into that good night."

"Visiting the Bird Feeder in Winter" was inspired by Robert Frost's "Stopping by Woods on a Snowy Evening," a modern Rubaiyat Stanza.

"Molly's Pantoum" was inspired by quotes from my dear friend Molly Marshall's holiday letters.

About the Author

Becky Ventura grew up in Omaha, Nebraska. She was a music education major in college, earning a Bachelor of Music in Education. Her post-graduate work was also in Education, with emphasis on Reading. She studied piano with acclaimed teacher/performer Audun Ravnan at the University of Nebraska-Lincoln. For over 30 years, Becky taught music in the public schools, retiring in 2018 from the Dearborn (Michigan) Public Schools. Over the years, she performed and directed choral concerts, accompanied and played solo piano in recitals. Becky received the Dearborn Mayor's Arts Educator Award, with US Congressional Recognition, in April 2019.

Becky is a member of the Poetry Society of Michigan. Her poems have been published on their forum. Her poem, "Winter Aspect," is included in the PSM 2021 Five Year Anthology. Becky enjoys reading the poetry of Judyth Hill, Billy Collins, Mary Oliver, Hedy Habra, Robert Frost and William Butler Yeats.

Becky is also a licensed Anusara™ Yoga Teacher. When attending an Anusara gathering at Estes Park in 2019, Becky had the good fortune of connecting with ebullient poet, Judyth Hill, there. Though Becky had written all her life, she never knew the joys of composing poetry until she met Judyth. Her studies with

Judyth continue. Becky has great enthusiasm for the artistry of poetry and music, and it is with a full heart that her poems are written.

Artist Statement:

I write from the heart, invoking whatever is living there to present itself, whether it's clear to me or not. I write to evoke remembrance in the reader; whatever that may be. Music influences how I write, my life has been ensconced in classical music, and its forms, phrases and expressions find their way into my poetry, much to my delight.